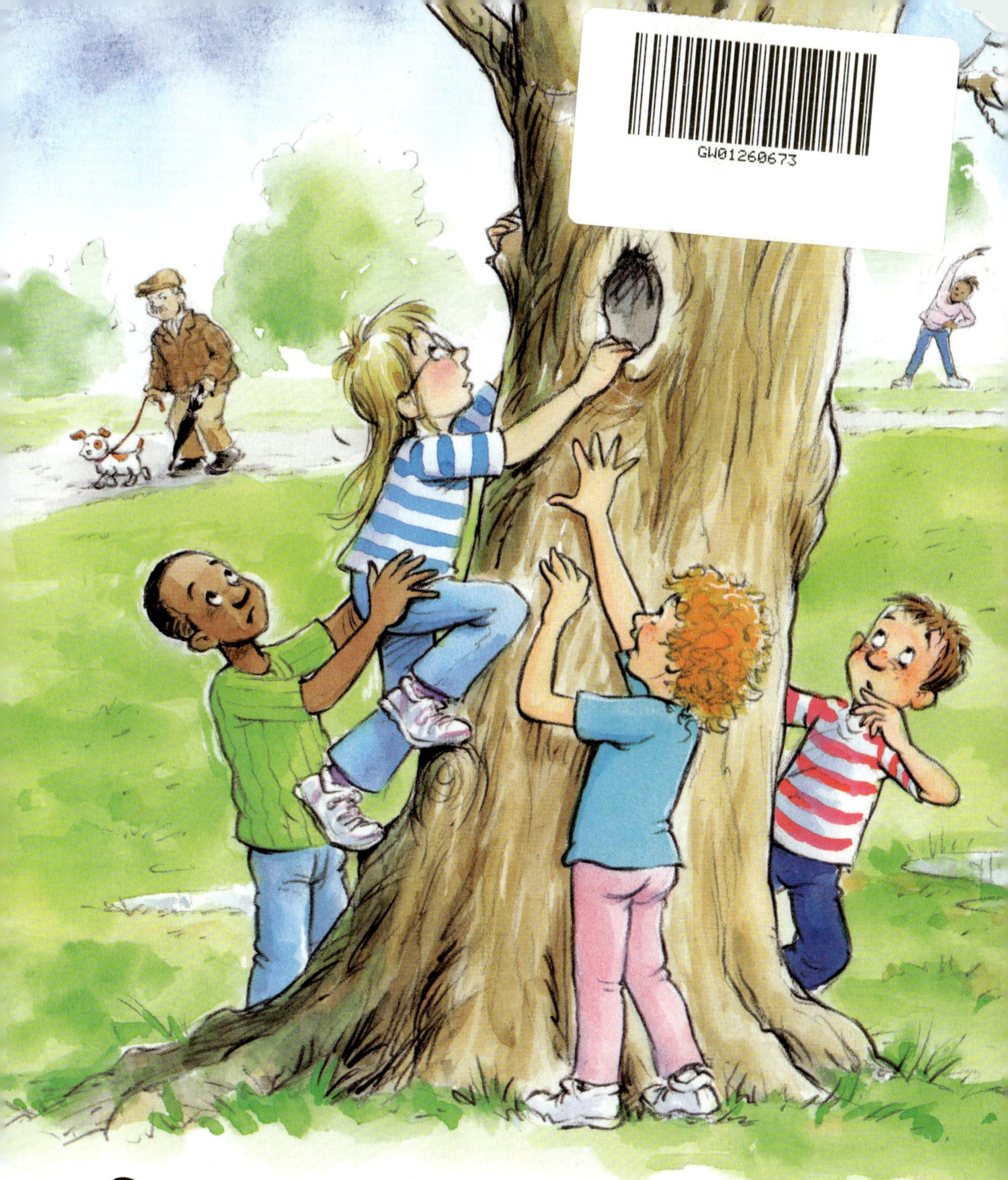

Sam is going up

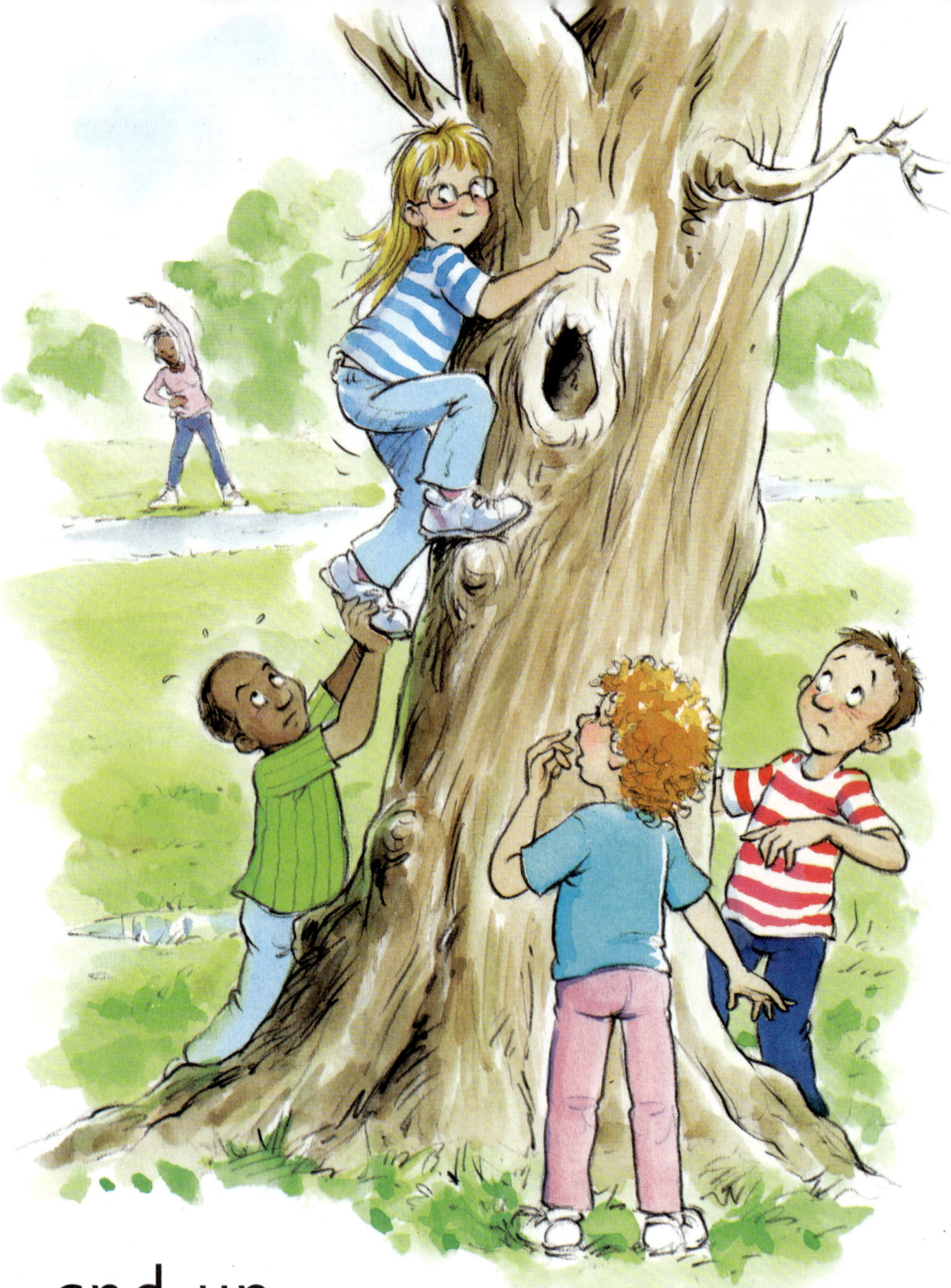

and up

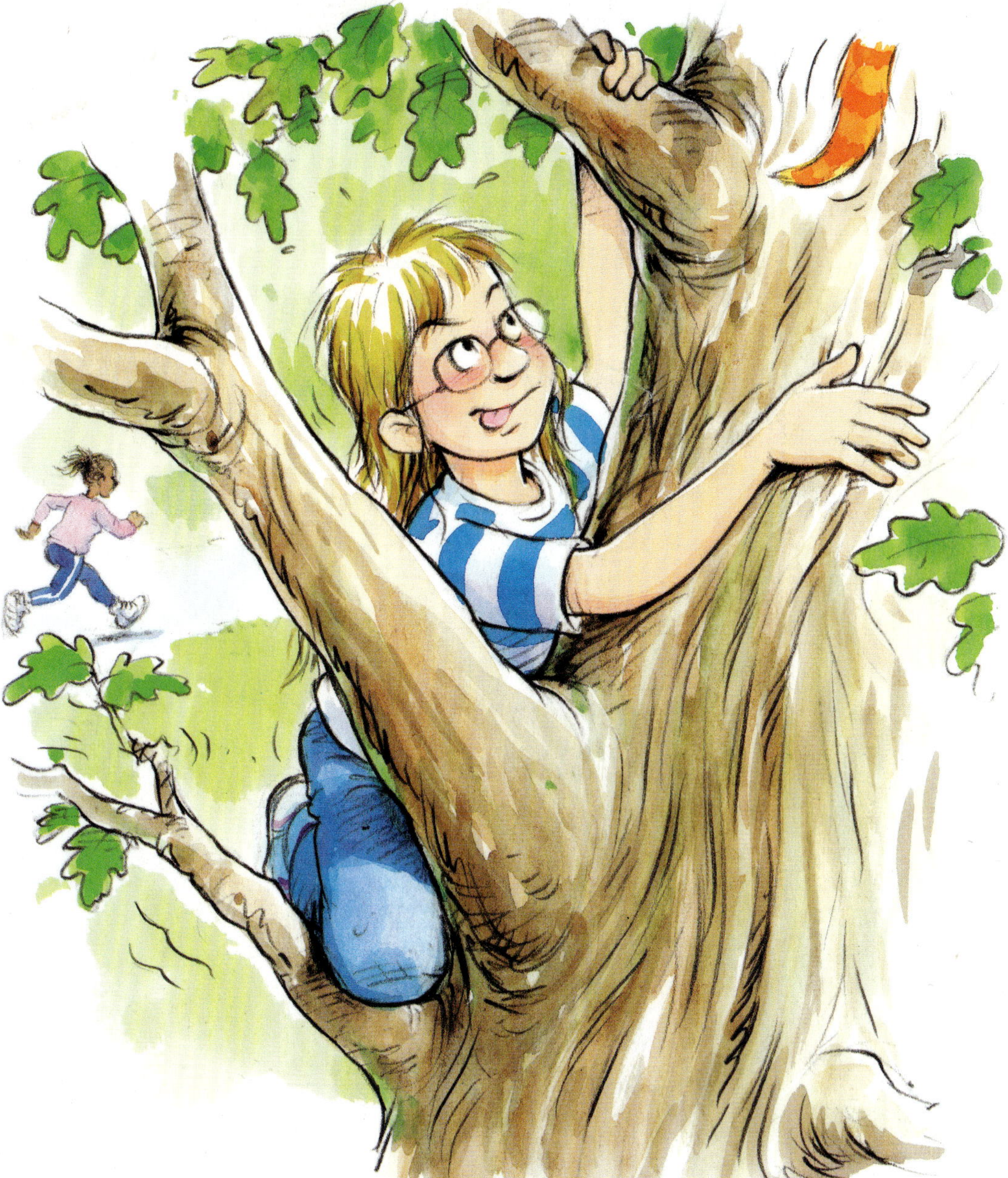

and up

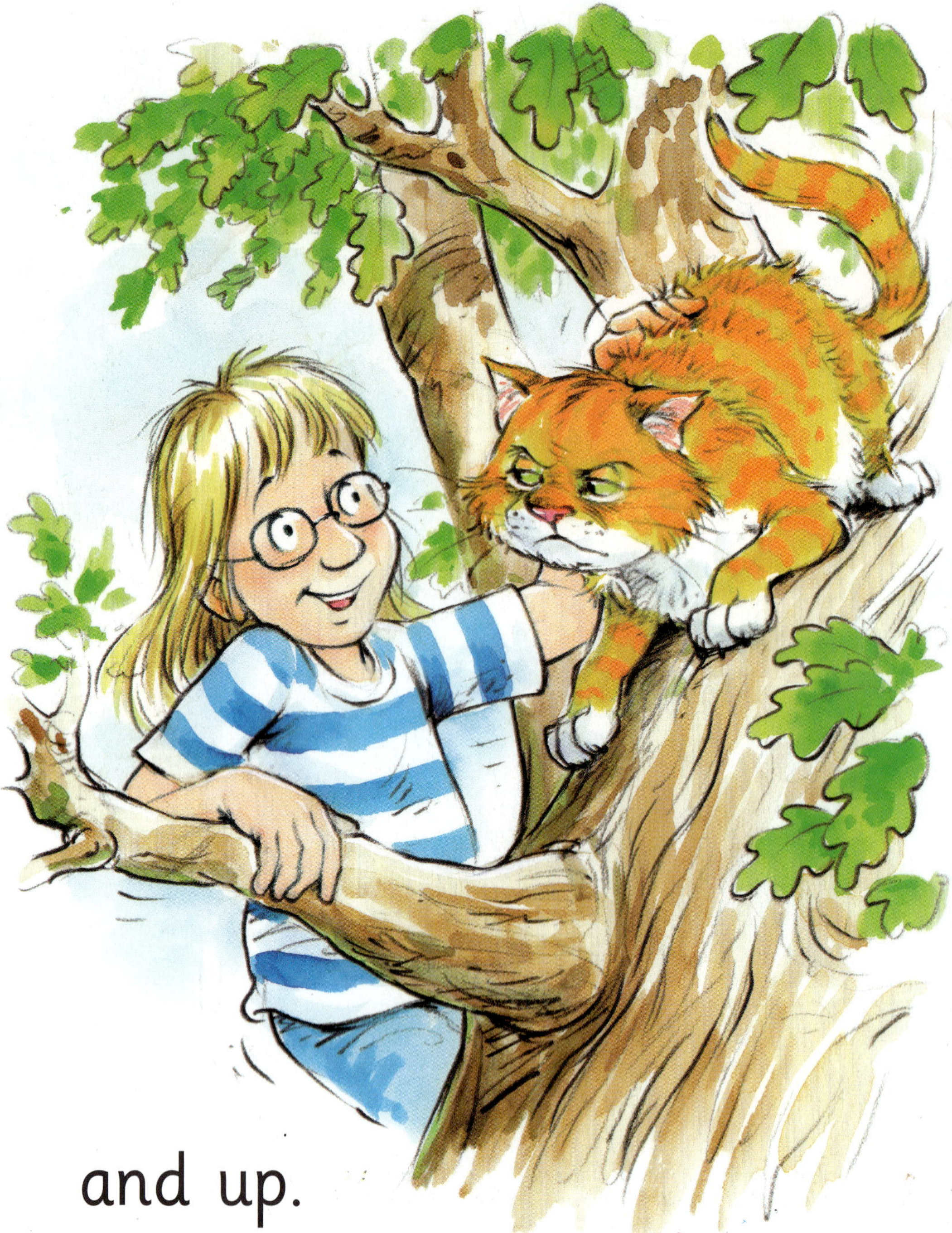

and up.

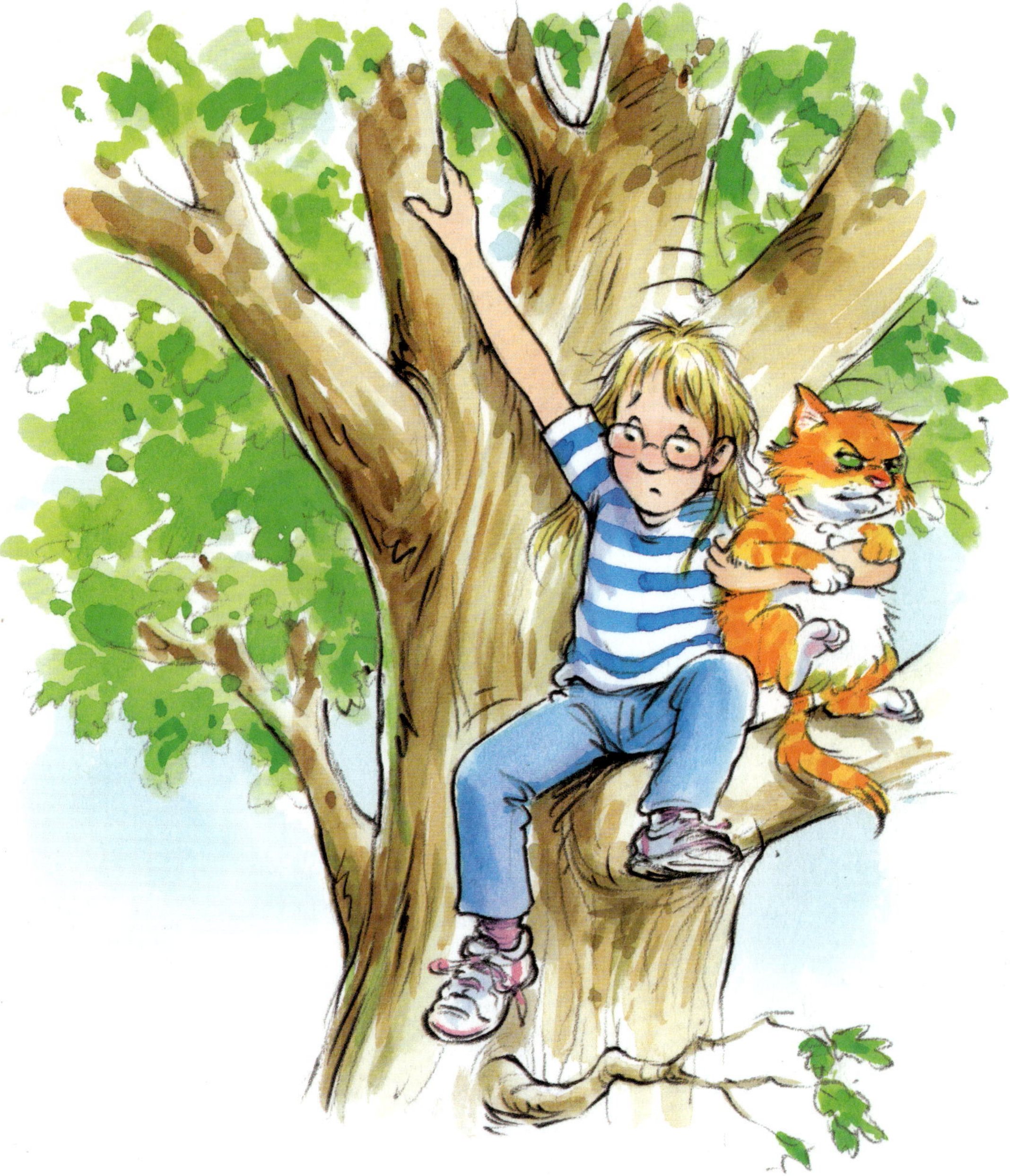

Sam is going down,

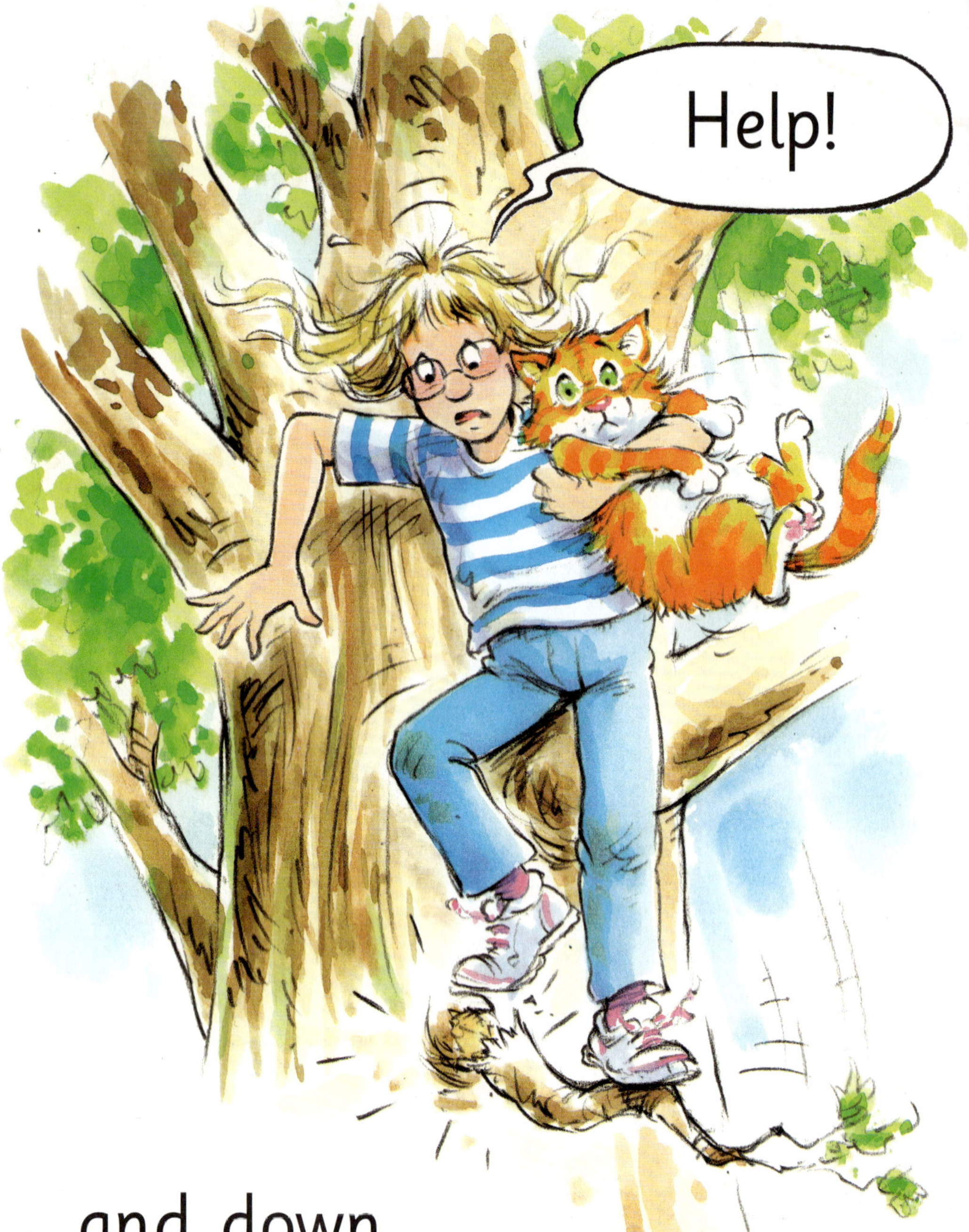

and down.

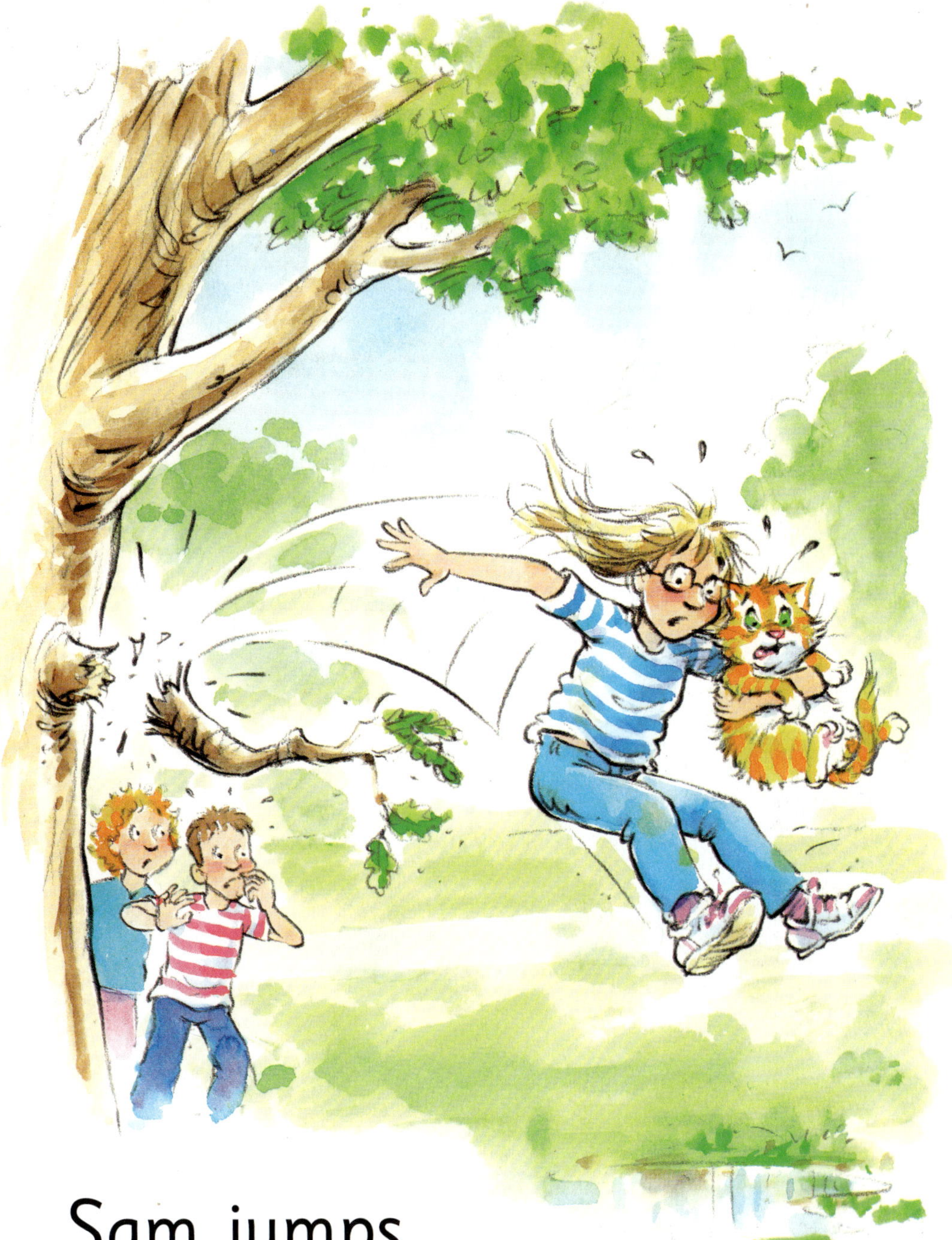

Sam jumps.

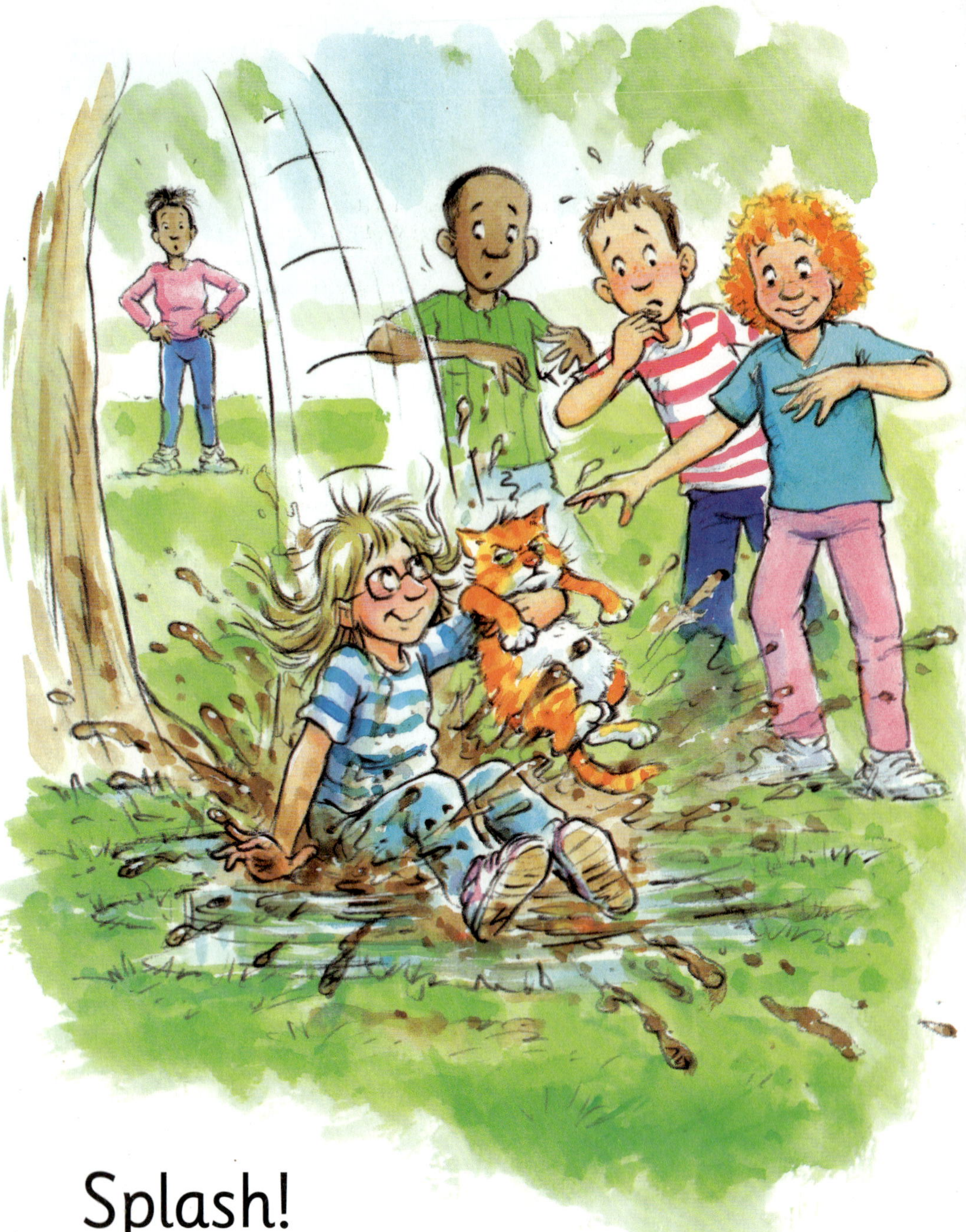

Splash!